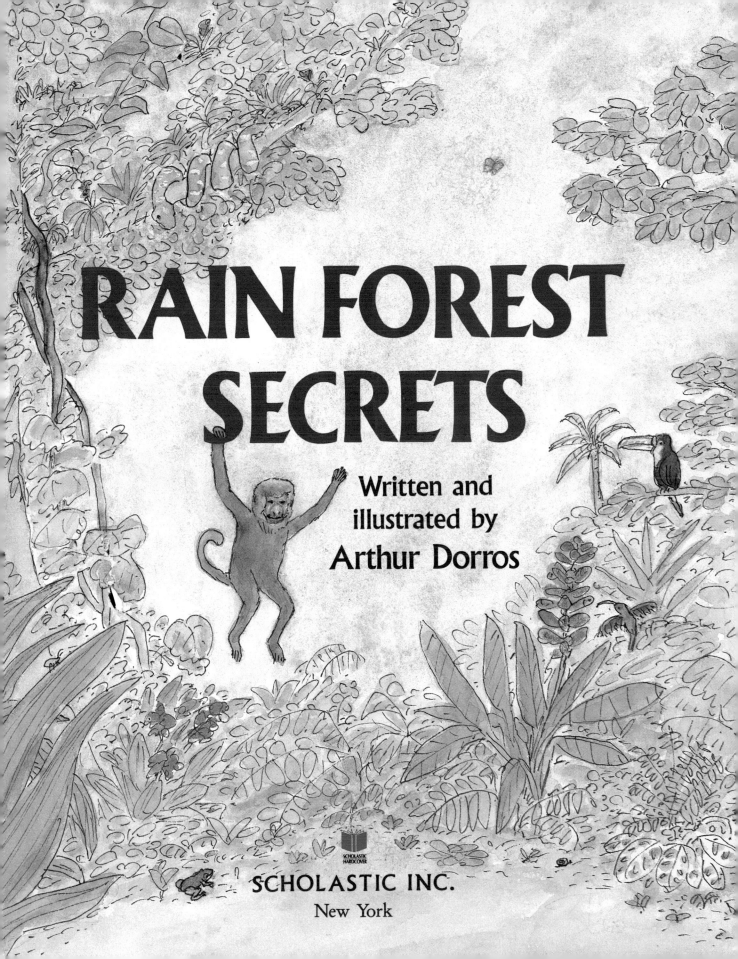

RAIN FOREST SECRETS

Written and
illustrated by
Arthur Dorros

SCHOLASTIC
HARDCOVER

SCHOLASTIC INC.
New York

To Brian C. and
his new cousin.

With special thanks to Gordon Orians,
Director, Institute for Environmental Studies,
University of Washington,
for reviewing text and art for this book.

Rain Forest Organizations

For more information about rain forests you can write to:

The Children's Rainforest **
P.O. Box 936
Lewiston, ME 04240

Conservation International
1015 18th St., NW
Suite 1000
Washington, DC 20036

Friends of the Earth/U.K. **
2628 Underwood Street
London N17JU United Kingdom

Global Tomorrow Coalition **
1325 G St., NW
Suite 915
Washington, DC 20005

International Union for the Conservation
of Nature and Natural Resources
Avenue Mont Blanc
1196 Gland
Switzerland

Missouri Botanical Garden **
P.O. Box 299
St. Louis, MO 63166

National Audubon Society **
801 Pennsylvania Ave., SE
Washington, DC 20003

National Wildlife Federation **
1400 16th St., NW
Washington, DC 20036-2266

National Zoological Park/
Smithsonian Institute **
Washington, DC 20008

The Nature Conservancy
1815 North Lynn Street
Arlington, VA 22209

Rainforest Action Network **
301 Broadway, Suite A
San Francisco, CA 94133

Smithsonian Tropical Research Institute **
APO
Miami, FL 34002-0011

The Wilderness Society
1400 Eye St., NW
Washington, DC 20005

Wildlife Conservation International
New York Zoological Society **
Bronx, NY 10460

World Wildlife Fund/Conservation Foundation **
1250 24th St., NW
Washington, DC 20037

World Wildlife Fund/U.K. **
Panda House
Godalming
Surrey GU7 IXR United Kingdom

**These organizations can provide
classroom materials.

There may be a "rain forest" close to your home.
Some zoos and museums have rain forest exhibits.

Copyright © 1990 by Arthur Dorros.

All rights reserved. Published by Scholastic Inc.

SCHOLASTIC HARDCOVER is a registered trademark of Scholastic Inc.

No part of this publication may be reproduced in whole or in
part, or stored in a retrieval system, or transmitted in any
form or by any means, electronic, mechanical, photocopying,
recording, or otherwise, without written permission of the
publisher. For information regarding permission, write to
Scholastic Inc., 730 Broadway, New York, NY 10003.

Library of Congress Cataloging-in-Publication Data

Dorros, Arthur.
Rain forest secrets/written and illustrated by Arthur Dorros.
p.   cm.
Summary: Describes the characteristics, various forms of plant and
animal life, and destruction of the world's rain forests.
ISBN 0-590-43369-5
1. Rain forest ecology—Juvenile literature. 2. Rain forests—
Juvenile literature. [1. Rain forests. 2. Rain forest ecology.
3. Ecology.] I. Title.
QH541.5.R27D67 1990
574.5'2642—dc20   89-49069
                                                   CIP
                                                   AC

12 11 10 9 8 7 6 5 4 3 2 1   0 1 2 3 4 5/9
Printed in the U.S.A.   36
First Scholastic printing, September 1990

Have you ever been to a rain forest?
If not, you've probably heard of rain forests.
Sometimes people call them "jungles."
In rain forests you can find
colorful birds calling,
monkeys leaping through trees,
giant flowers—
more kinds of plants and animals
than anywhere else on earth.

Most rain forests are *tropical rain forests*.
They are in the tropics, near the equator,
where it is warm year-round.

From the air, a lowland tropical rain forest
looks like a green ocean. It stays green all year.

A rain forest is a good place for growing plants,
with year-round warm temperatures of 70–90°F (22°–32°C)
and plenty of sunlight and water.

Rain forests get from six feet to more than thirty feet
of rain a year. Most afternoons it rains—often very hard.
Inches of rain can fall in just a few hours.

Plants soak up much of the water that falls in the
rain forest, but some of the water is carried away by rivers.

The Amazon river, flowing through the biggest
rain forest in the world, carries one-sixth of
all the earth's water that flows into oceans.
Along the river, trees and plants form a
wall of green. The rain forest's rich plant life
provides food and homes to an incredible number
of mammals, birds, and insects.

Fruit-eating macaws flap into the sky.
Fish gobble fruit that splatters into the water.
A family of giant otters, as big as people, splashes
in the river, playing, and chasing fish to eat.
A caiman floats in the river, looking like a log.

By the riverbank, where there is plenty of sunlight, rain forest plants grow thick and tangled.

In the shade of the large trees that form a *canopy* over most of the rain forest, not as many plants can grow. Trees block the sunlight as well as the wind. The air is still.

The dark forest floor stays warm and wet. It is carpeted with a thin layer of dead, wrinkled brown leaves.

At first it is hard to see the life on the forest floor. But bits of green leaves are moving. The leaves are being carried underground by leaf-cutting ants. The ants chew and spit out the leaves to make gardens where they raise mushroom-like fungi to eat.

There are more ants than any other creature in the rain forest. There can be forty kinds of ants all in one tree.

In the heat and moisture of the rain forest floor,
things rot quickly. Dead wood and leaves rot fast
with the help of bacteria, fungi, and insects,
particularly termites.

The decayed plants provide nutrients to the soil that
help plants grow. But the nutrient-rich, or food-rich,
soil is only a thin layer on the rain forest floor.
The trees and plants quickly soak up the soil food
with shallow surface roots. *Buttresses* stick out from
some tree trunks, and help support the shallow-rooted
tall trees. Other trees send *stilt roots* into
the forest floor.

Stilt roots

Buttress

Big animals also make the forest floor their home.
A giant anteater slurps up a lunch of termites with its
long, sticky tongue. Tapirs, peccaries, and deer chew
on plants and seeds in the Amazon rain forest,
while jaguars watch.

There are different large animals in other rain forests.
Leopards live in African and Asian rain forests.
Tigers can be found in Asia.
The big animals on the forest floor are rarely seen by people.
They stay hidden in the rain forest.

Anteater

Peccaries

Tapir

Curassow

Armadillo

Brocket
deer

Jaguar

Paca

Of the 30 million or so kinds of plants and animals
that scientists believe live on earth, more than half
live in rain forests, even though rain forests cover only
a small amount of the earth. Most of the plants and
animals in the rain forest have not even been discovered
by scientists yet.

Listen, it is quiet. At first all you can hear is the
pat pat pat of raindrops dripping from
the leaf tips above. A bird calls, yodeling a song.
Then *thud!* a piece of fruit falls nearby.
A monkey is dropping part of its breakfast.
A group of spider monkeys dangles and leaps
high up in the trees, rustling the leaves.

There are many layers of life in the rain forest.
Each layer provides a different kind of home
to the plants and animals that live there.
The top layer of trees, called the *canopy,*
is a thick garden of leaves basking in the sunlight.

The canopy buzzes, chirps, and howls with life.
Bees, hummingbirds, butterflies, and bats
swoop from flower to flower, drinking nectar
and helping to pollinate the flowers.
Pollinated flowers can become fruit that will
be eaten by parrots, toucans, insects, bats,
monkeys, and other animals.

Pollen

Animals help spread seeds around the rain forest.
Some of the seeds fall to the forest floor.
A few will grow into seedlings of the trees
that make up the canopy. Other seeds fall onto
branches of the trees.

Canopy trees are covered with plants that
grow in the sunlight. These plants, called *epiphytes*,
or air plants, hang onto the trees. Air plants soak up
food and water with their leaves and roots.
Some hold pools of rainwater in their leaves
and eat insects that fall into the water.
There are other plants, such as vines and figs,
whose roots drop all the way to the forest floor
to pick up nutrients.

Each plant flower in the canopy has a specific color,
scent, or shape that attracts different animals.

Katydid

Orchid

Bromeliad

Air plants are home to many animals.
Tree frogs grow up in treetop air plant pools.
Insects like the praying mantis disguise themselves
as flowers, twigs, or leaves to hide from birds and
other predators. A lizard stops to take a drink.
Some animals spend their whole lives in the canopy
and never touch the ground.

Fig roots

Moth

Praying mantis

Most trees in the canopy are 60–120 feet tall.
But giant *emergent* trees grow even higher.
A harpy eagle lands in an emergent tree
towering above the canopy. The eagle sits in its watchtower
island and tries to spot a sloth or monkey to eat.

There are many sloths in the canopy, but they are
hard to see. Sloths don't move much and they
are greenish. They are covered with green algae.
The algae, and keeping still, help a sloth and its baby
hide from the eagle and other predators.

Sloths spend most of their lives upside down,
hanging from branches and eating leaves.
Sloths even sleep hanging upside down.
A sloth does everything...slowly....
It can take a month for a sloth to digest a meal.

Not all the animals of the rain forest move
as slowly or are as quiet as the peaceful sloth.
A *ROARRR* booms through the canopy.
It's a howler monkey, howling a warning.
A toucan crashes through leaves in the *understory.*

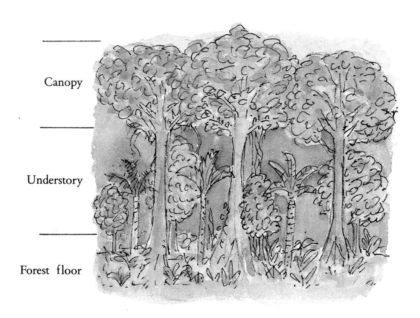

Canopy

Understory

Forest floor

The understory is the layer of smaller trees
and plants that grows below the canopy.
It is shadowy, but full of life, too.
Woody vines called *lianas* creep toward
the light in the canopy.
An ocelot, a cat smaller than a jaguar,
naps in an understory tree.

Clear-wing butterflies become
almost invisible in the shadows.
A boa constrictor tries to blend into
the trees by hanging like a liana.
Snakes are not often seen in the rain forest
during the day because they hide so well.

Liana

Iguana

Ferns and palms that look like they could be
from the age of dinosaurs reach for light.
Rain forests were around in the time of dinosaurs.
One reason tropical rain forests contain so
many forms of life may be because rain forests
have been around for so long.

Today in the warm rain forest, a hungry iguana climbs a tree to dine on fruit. People climb here, too. They harvest Brazil nuts, cashews, and the cacao that's used to make chocolate.

Pineapple

African violet

Papaya

Avocado

Cacao

Orange

Bromeliad

Peppers

Peanuts

Banana

Coconut

Pepper

Christmas cactus

Lemon

Periwinkle

People who live in the rain forest use thousands of kinds of plants for food and medicines. Bananas, avocados, pineapples, peppers, and peanuts are just a few of the foods that first came from rain forests. You may even have a little bit of living rain forest in your home. Many plants that first came from rain forests are now grown as house plants.

Some diseases have been cured with rain forest plant medicines. About one-fourth of all the medicines we use come from rain forest plants. A cure for certain types of cancer was discovered in a rain forest periwinkle flower. People who live in rain forests grow dozens of kinds of plants together in gardens in rain forest clearings.

There are clearings where big old trees have fallen, too.
Tree seedlings that were growing in the shadows
now have light to grow tall. The forest is constantly changing.
In old garden clearings, or where trees have fallen,
new plants shoot up, and the rain forest continues to grow.

But where a lot of land is cleared,
the rain forest dies. Thousands of acres a day
are being cleared for raising cattle or for farming.
Other land is cleared of trees for making lumber
or to build roads, mines, and dams.

Without plants to hold it, what little food
there is in the soil quickly washes away.
The rivers fill with mud. There is
little to eat. Fruit-eating fish and other
animals help spread the seeds of trees.
If there are no seeds to spread, new trees
don't grow. Once one kind of plant or animal dies
in the rain forest, others that depend on it die, too.

Some scientists think that destroying the rain
forests will make the whole earth's climate warmer.
The warming is called the *greenhouse effect.*

Rain forest trees and plants hold moisture.
They breathe back into the air, or *transpire,*
up to three-fourths of all the rain they get.
This causes more rain. Cutting down rain forests
reduces the amount of rain the earth receives.
The land can become dry and barren.

When an old rain forest is destroyed, it may never recover. Rain forests have taken millions of years to become what they are.

But there are ways to use products from the rain forest without destroying it. Trees can be grown on land that has already been cleared. Rubber tappers gather liquid rubber—*latex*—from the same trees, year after year. Fruits, nuts, and plants for medicines can be gathered without hurting the rain forest.

There are other kinds of rain forests
besides lowland rain forests like the Amazon.
Montane rain forests grow on mountainsides.
The slightly cooler air of the mountains
can turn the moisture from the rain forest into mist.
Some montane rain forests are called cloud forests
because they are clouded in mist so often.
Gorillas live in the misty montane rain forests of Africa.
Gorillas are peaceful and shy, and spend their days
munching on rain forest greens and fruit.

Some tropical forests get more rain than others.
There are tropical forests with long dry seasons.
Mangrove forests grow along the sea, where
they soak up sea water, so they stay wet year-round.
Roots of the mangrove trees hold soil and keep it from
getting washed away. Crabs, frogs, turtles, insects,
birds, proboscis monkeys, and tree-climbing fish
live together in an Asian mangrove forest.

Most of the rain forests of the world are
tropical rain forests, close to the equator.
But there are also temperate rain forests in cool,
but not freezing, areas.

Temperate rain forests grow along the west coast
of North America, from northern California to
British Columbia, Canada, and Alaska.
Some of these rain forests get over fifteen feet
of rain a year! Temperate rain forests do not have
as many kinds of plants or animals as tropical rain
forests, but they are rich with life.

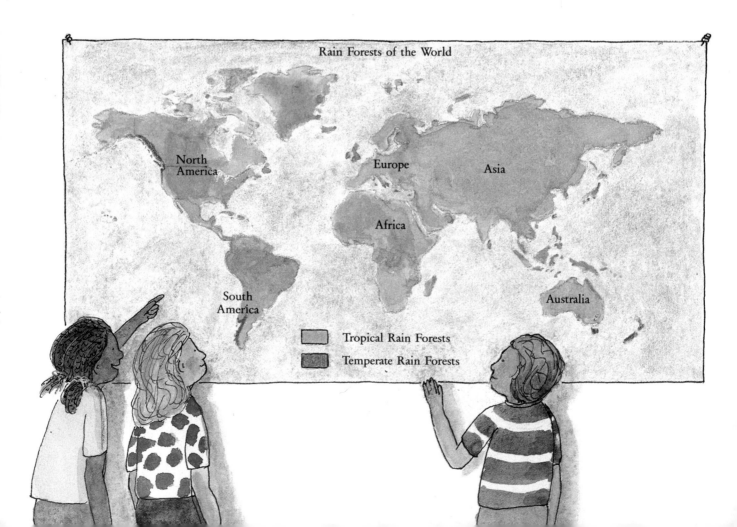

Ancient giant trees, over one thousand years old, grow in temperate rain forests called *old-growth forests*. The biggest trees on earth tower here. Sequoia trees can grow to over three hundred feet tall—higher than some city apartment buildings.

Douglas fir, cedar, hemlock, and spruce trees can top two hundred feet, and be thirty-five feet around!

Bears, cougars, deer, porcupines, skunks, and raccoons live on the forest floor.

Eagles, woodpeckers, owls, flying squirrels, bats, insects, and mice live in the understory and treetop canopy.

Lichens, ferns, and mosses, the air plants of the temperate forest, carpet tree branches, catching rainfall in the canopy.

Woodpeckers *tap tap tap*, looking for insects in the trees.

A woodpecker family carves its own home in a dead standing tree, called a *snag*. Other birds and animals move into the woodpecker nest when the woodpeckers move out.

When a snag, or an old tree, crashes down,
it opens the forest floor to light.

The fallen tree is a storehouse of food and water for
wood-eating beetles, carpenter ants, termites, fungi,
spiders, salamanders, voles, mice, and shrews.
Voles may be tiny, but they help giant trees grow.
Voles eat fungi, and spread fungus spores to grow
on tree roots. The fungi help tree roots gather
the nitrogen trees need for food.

Carpenter ants

Salamander

Vole

Shrew

Beetle

New plants and trees sprout on rotting logs.
It can take three hundred years for a giant log to rot!
Sometimes in an old-growth forest you can see
a neat row of trees. The trees started as seedlings
that sprouted on a rotting log years ago.
Out of the thousands of seeds that fall from
one tree, only a few grow into seedlings.
Only one of the seedlings may live
to become a giant tree.

Old-growth rain forests help keep water clean.
Water reaching the forest floor filters
through decaying logs, branches, and leaves.
Fallen trees in streams help filter water, too.
Pools by the logs are good places
for baby salmon and trout to grow.

Where old-growth rain forests are cut down,
streams and rivers flow muddy.
Most of our old-growth temperate rain forests
have already been cleared. For every five giant trees
that were once in our forests, only one is left.
But the old giants are still being cut down.

An area of tropical rain forest about the size of
four city blocks is being destroyed every minute.
If this continues, there may be no old rain forests
left in less than seventy-five years.
But there are people all over the world
working to help save rain forests.

As jaguars, eagles, gorillas, and bears watch silently, people explore the glittering wet forests. For every kind of plant or animal that we know of in rain forests, scientists think there are at least twenty yet to learn about. New plants we can use for food and medicine are still being discovered.

Rain forests hold many secrets for all of us. Who knows what *you* might find in a rain forest?

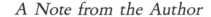

A Note from the Author

When I was four years old, I sat on the tail of a real alligator—ten feet long. Fortunately, the alligator had just been fed. Surrounded by palm trees, I felt I was in the jungle. This was the beginning of my interest in the tropics. Later I was able to visit real rain forests around the world.

I've seen elephants in Asian rain forests, (where there are also flying frogs and lizards); monkeys, birds, and butterflies in Indonesia; parrots and flying opossums in Australia; toucans, agoutis, snakes, spider monkeys, and thousands of kinds of insects in Central and South America. In the temperate rain forest, near where I live, I've watched bears and otters, eagles and jumping salmon, porcupines, and a completely white deer, which looked magical.

There is so much to see, smell, touch, and hear in rain forests—I'm always excited about what I'll find. But I'm concerned about whether or not there will be any old rain forests left. Here in the Pacific Northwest, old giants are cut for lumber, even though there are lots of other trees to harvest. Tropical rain forests are being cut down and burned. I hope there will be some ancient rain forest left for all of us. And if you haven't already, I hope you will have a chance to visit a rain forest.

An experiment: If you would like to get an idea of how much life there is in the rain forest, you can look in your own backyard. Select a small area, perhaps the size of a shoe box. Look very carefully and count all the different kinds of life there—plants and animals. See how much you can find. The same amount of space in a rain forest would have ten times as many kinds of life!

If you would like to find out more about rain forests, or how to help save them, there is a list of places you can write to on page two of this book.